Disney's Bonkers JOKE BOOK

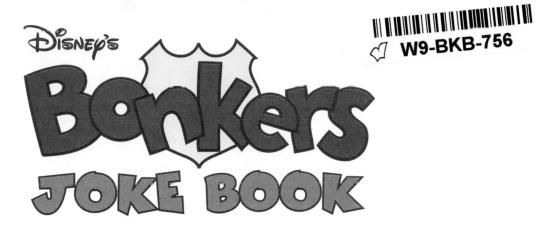

By Linda Williams Aber
Illustrated by Darrell Baker

W9-BKB-756

A GOLDEN BOOK • NEW YORK

Golden Books Publishing Company, Inc., Racine, Wisconsin 53404

© Disney Enterprises, Inc. All rights reserved. Printed in the U.S.A. No part of this book may be reproduced or copied in any form without written permission from the copyright owner. GOLDEN BOOKS & DESIGN™, A GOLDEN BOOK®, A GOLDEN LOOK-LOOK® BOOK, A GOLDEN LOOK-LOOK BOOK AND DESIGN®, and the distinctive gold spine are trademarks of Golden Books Publishing Company, Inc. Library of Congress Catalog Card Number: 94-77007 ISBN: 0-307-12884-9   MCMXCVII

TOTALLY BONKERS!

MARILYN: Why is the baseball player going to jail?

CHIEF KANIFKY: He was caught stealing second base.

What do you call someone who steals windshields?

A windshield swiper.

SPOTLIGHT ON BONKERS

Did you hear about the actor who fell through the floor?

It was just a stage he was going through!

BONKERS: I was once in a cartoon called "Breakfast in Bed."

JITTERS: Did you have a big role?

BONKERS: No, just some toast and jam.

What do cows do on Saturday night?

They go to the moo-vies!

BONKERS: Have you ever seen me on TV?

FAN: Yes, on and off.

BONKERS: How did you like me?

FAN: Off!

Did you hear about the actor who does bird impressions?

He eats worms and flies.

TV STUDIO

STAGE DOOR

A film about a rock singer is a

groovy movie!

TANYA: Waiter, is there spaghetti on the menu?

WAITER: No, madam. I wiped it off.

DETECTIVE PIQUEL: Waiter, why is my food so messy?

WAITER: You asked me to step on it, sir!

A frightened chef is a

shook cook!

TANYA'S TRUNKFUL OF LAUGHS

Why did Tanya paint her toenails red?

So she could hide in the strawberry patch!

How do you keep an elephant from charging?

Refuse to take her credit card!

Why are elephants big, gray, and wrinkled?

Because if they were small, white, and smooth, they would be eggs!

Why do elephants have trunks?

They'd look silly with suitcases!

What do elephants have that no other animals have?

Baby elephants!

An elephant's shovel is a bigger digger!

What's black and white, and black and white, and black and white?

A zebra caught in a revolving door!

What's black and white, and black and white, and green?

A penguin and a skunk fighting over a pickle!

A talkative penguin is a

wordy birdie!

PIQUEL'S PACK OF PICKLE JOKES

What does a pickle say when it wants to play cards?

"Dill me in!"

How does a ghost eat a pickle?

By goblin' it!

What instrument did the pickle play in the quartet?

The piccolo!

Why did the cucumber call 911?

He was in a pickle!

A five-cent cucumber is a nickel pickle!

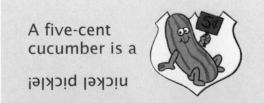

BONKERS' CORNIEST JOKES

How can you divide seven
potatoes among four people?

Mash them!

What do you call a bunch
of carrots that talk back?

Fresh vegetables!

Why should you never tell secrets in a cornfield?

Because it's all ears!

What did one tomato say to the other?

You go ahead, I'll ketchup!

A nervous celery stalk is an

edgy veggie!

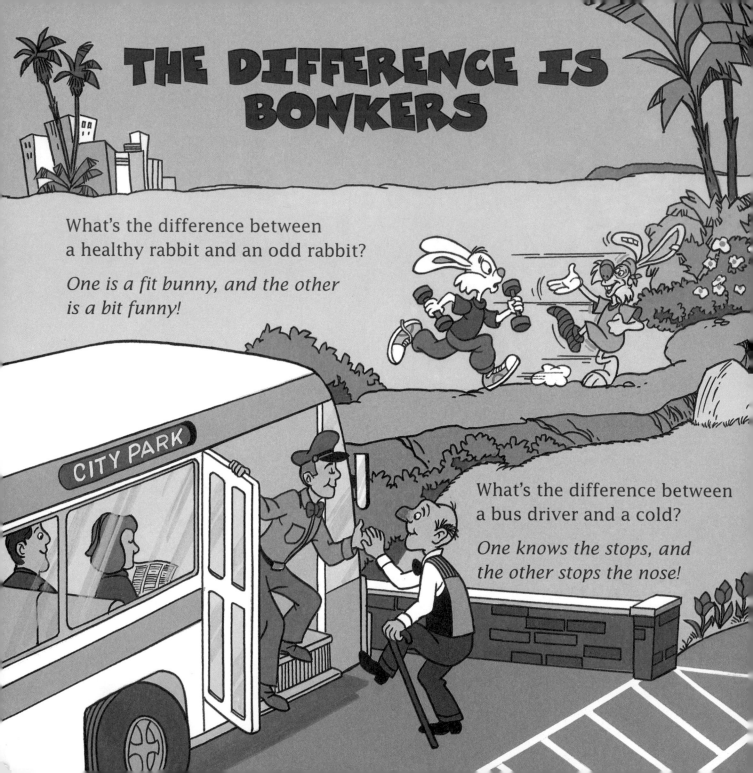

What's the difference between a hill and a pill?

One is hard to get up, and the other is hard to get down!

What's the difference between a hairy dog and a painter?

One sheds his coat, and the other coats his shed!

MARILYN: What's the difference between an elephant and a mailbox?

DETECTIVE PIQUEL: I don't know.

MARILYN: Ha! Remind me never to ask you to mail a letter!

A rabbit pays his bills with

bunny money!

WHAT DOES BONKERS CALL IT?

What does Bonkers call a kid with a dictionary in his back pocket?

Smarty-pants!

What does Bonkers call an American drawing?

A Yankee Doodle!

What does Bonkers call a cat that eats lemons?

A sour puss!

What does Bonkers call the life story of a car?

An auto-biography!

What does Bonkers call two spiders who have just gotten married?

Newlywebs!

A meeting of dogs is a bow-wow-wow!

BONKERS' GRAPEVINE

Have you heard about the prisoner who found a rope?

Skip it!

Have you heard about the prisoner who stole some meat?

He was a hamburglar!

Have you heard about the prisoner who robbed a music store?

He got caught with the lute!

Have you heard about the prisoner who ate a candle?

He wanted a light snack!

A robber who gets caught in five minutes is a brief thief!

RANCHER: Do you want a saddle with or without a horn?

CHIEF KANIFKY: Without. You don't seem to have too much traffic here!

What's as big as a prize steer and weighs nothing?

A prize steer's shadow!

A fake horse is a

phony pony!

CASE CLOSED

FALL APART RABBIT: How can I tell if a cat burglar's been in my house?

DETECTIVE PIQUEL: Your cat will be gone!

What did Jitters say when he walked into the police station?

Ouch!

MIRANDA: I think you should take something for that cold.

BONKERS: Great! I'll take the rest of the week off!